BAXTER

J.C. RYLE

BAXTER

FOREWORD BY TIM COOPER

H&E
Publishing

Baxter

Copyright © 2018 H&E Publishing
www.hesedandemet.com

All Scripture quotations are taken and adapted from the King James Version.

Published by: H&E Publishing, Peterborough, Canada
Editors: Chance Faulkner and Corey M. K. Hughes
Cover image original drawing: Richard Baxter, 2018 Tyler Swaffield

Source in Public Domain: J. C. Ryle, *The Priest, the Puritan and the Preacher*. Published by New York: Robert Carter & Brothers, No. 285 Broadway, 1856

First Edition, 2018
Printed in Canada

Paperback ISBN: 978-1-989174-00-5
ePub ISBN: 978-1-989174-06-7

Contents

Publisher's Note

In this edition, the punctuation and capitalization have been modernized, some archaic words have been updated, and a few other slight editorial changes made. Any significant changes note the original in the footnotes.

Acknowledgments

Thank you, Bennett Rogers for your contribution to this work. To Benjamin Inglis for proofreading, and many thanks to Tim Cooper for not only his contribution but also his expertise and input.

SERIES PREFACE
WHO IS J.C. RYLE (1816–1900)?

Bennett W. Rogers

J.C. Ryle was born and raised in a wealthy but unspiritual home.[1] He distinguished himself academically and athletically at Eton and Oxford. He experienced an evangelical conversion in his final year at university, the account of which has achieved a semi-legendary status among evangelicals—a testimony to the power of the public reading of Scripture.[2] Shortly thereafter, his

---

[1] For a life of Ryle, see Eric Russell, *J.C. Ryle: That Man of Granite with the Heart of a Child* (Fearn, Scotland: Christian Focus Publications, 2008); John Murray, Iain H. Murray, *J.C. Ryle: Prepared to Stand Alone* (Edinburgh, UK: Banner of Truth Trust, 2016); or my new intellectual biography of Ryle entitled *John Charles Ryle: The Man, His Ministry, and His Message* (Grand Rapids: Reformation Heritage Books, 2018).

[2] Around the time of his examinations, John Charles attended Carfax Church, formally known as St. Martin's, feeling somewhat depressed and discouraged. The reader of the lesson made some lengthy pauses when he came to verse 8: "By grace—are ye saved—through faith—and that, not of yourselves—it is the gift of God." This unusual and emphatic reading of Ephesians 2:8 made a

father's bankruptcy ruined the family, ended his political career before it started, and forced him into the ministry of the Church of England. Although he initially became a clergyman because he felt "shut up to it," Ryle quickly gained a reputation for being a powerful preacher, diligent pastor, popular author, and effective controversialist. He rose through the evangelical ranks to become the undisputed leader and party spokesman—the first to hold that distinction since Charles Simeon (1759-1836). He became the first bishop of Liverpool in 1880 at an age (64) when many clergymen contemplate retirement, and served as the chief pastor of the second city of the British Empire until his death in 1900.

Ryle is probably best remembered as a writer of tracts, commentaries, and devotional works, and deservedly so. His tracts continue to be distributed. His commentaries on the gospels—*Expository Thoughts on the Gospels*—are still read by pastors and laymen alike. His practical writings, such as *Old Paths*, *Practical Religion*, and the *Upper Room* have remained popular with evangelical readers for well over a century. And *Holiness: Its Nature, Hindrances, Difficulties, and Roots* has become a modern spiritual classic. J. C. Ryle was also keenly interested in church history. In fact, he wrote twenty five short biographies of important figures in English church history and published a number of popular historical

---

tremendous impact on him and led to his own evangelical conversion.

works about the English Reformation.[3] Ryle believed that church history is not merely interesting—it is instructive. It is nothing less than "history teaching by examples."

---

[3] Ryle wrote biographical sketches of the following persons: George Whitefield, John Wesley, William Grimshaw, William Romaine, Daniel Rowlands, John Berridge, Henry Venn, Samuel Walker, James Hervey, Augustus Toplady, Fletcher of Madeley, John Wycliffe, John Rogers, John Hooper, Rowland Taylor, Hugh Latimer, John Bradford, Nicholas Ridley, Samuel Ward, Archbishop Laud, Richard Baxter, William Gurnall, James II and the Seven Bishops, Thomas Manton, and Colonel Robert Holden. For Ryle's works on the English Reformation see: *Lessons from English Church History*, *What Do We Owe the Reformation*, and *Why Were Our Reformers Burned*.

FOREWORD

Tim Cooper

Though he died over three hundred years ago, Richard Baxter remains a man to be heeded. He lived in a different age but it is one that speaks to the particular deficiencies, weaknesses and temptations of our own day and culture. That is first of all because Baxter was a Puritan, and Puritans were serious about God, and serious with God. They were also shrewd interpreters of the human heart, and despite the enormous differences between their times and ours, the human heart is still "deceitful above all things and beyond cure. Who can understand it?" (Jer. 17:9). Part of the Puritan project was to understand the human heart and to bring correction to what is broken and twisted. They were serious about sin but they were serious, too, about joy, about salvation, about a life of integrity and faithful devotion lived out in the world. They were not ones to be easily tamed by the seductions of entertainment, sports, games and empty self-promotion.

Richard Baxter embodies all of these qualities and was one of the most significant English Puritans of the seventeenth century. He published around 150 books, some of them very long, all of them serious, weighty and needful. He never wrote anything, he said, except out of "necessity." For more than a decade he engaged in effective and innovative pastoral ministry in his parish of Kidderminster. He developed a model of serious pastoral concern that he published in one his classic texts, *The Reformed Pastor*, which is still in print today. That model was copied in other places and may have led to genuine reformation if the Puritan cause had not been cut short by the restoration of the English monarchy in 1662 and the resulting settlement that shut them out of ministry in the Church of England.

That bitter experience, Baxter's earlier traumatic experience of the English civil wars, and his lifelong suffering from ill health consistently drove him to look beyond this world for joy and happiness. For him, the stakes were always nothing less than eternal. He preached "as a dying man to dying men," and when he was allowed to preach no longer he turned to the pen. His *Christian Directory*, published in 1673 and around one million words in length, was a practical guide for Christian living in every conceivable circumstance of life during our pilgrimage here on earth. This world is not our home. Another of his classic works, *The Saints' Everlasting Rest*, urges the reader to contemplate heaven as the true measure of life, one that puts this current world in its proper place. As he explained in *The Crucifying of the World by the Cross of Christ*, "If the *world* would know its own place, it might be esteemed and *used* in its place; but if it will needs pretend to be what it is not, and will promise to do what it cannot, and so would not only be *used* but *enjoyed*, we must take it for a deceiver, and rise up against it with the greatest detestation. For else it will be the certain damnation of our souls. For he that has a wrong *End*, is wrong in all the *means*."[4] Baxter was always clear on the right ends, and the proper means to those ends. He orients us in the life of faith in a way that will expose the dangers we face in our twenty-first century culture. His voice speaks still and it is worth heeding, if we will listen.

Tim Cooper
Associate Professor of Church History
University of Otago, New Zealand

---

[4] *The Practical Works of the Late Reverend and Pious Mr. Richard Baxter* (London: Thomas Parkhurst, Jonathan Robinson and John Lawrence, 1707), III, 450.

INTRODUCTION

I must ask you to look back to times long gone by—to look back to the seventeenth century.[5] I feel this is rather a bold request to make. Progress is the order of the day in which you live. "Go ahead" has become a familiar expression wherever English is spoken. "Forward" is the motto of the times. Few are willing to look back.

But there are subjects about which it is well to look behind us. There are matters in which a knowledge of the past may teach us wisdom for the present and the future. The history of religion is pre-eminently such a subject and matter. Steam, electricity, railways, and gas, have made a wonderful difference in the temporal condition of mankind in the last two hundred years. But all this time the Bible and the hearts of men have remained unaltered. That which men did and thought in religious matters two hundred years ago, they are capable of doing and thinking again. What they thought

---

[5] Original: back some two hundred years.

1

and did in England, in the seventeenth century, it is well to know.

And just as there are subjects about which it is wise to look behind us, so also there are times long gone by which deserve our special attention. There are times when the character of a nation receives an indelible impression from events which take place in a single generation. There have been times when the dearest privileges of a people have been brought to the birth, and called into vigorous existence, through the desperate agony of civil war and religious strife. Such, I take leave to say, were the times of which I am about to write.[6] To no times are Englishmen so deeply indebted for their civil and religious liberty as the times in which Baxter lived. To no men do they owe such an unpaid debt of gratitude as they do to that noble host, of which Baxter was a standard-bearer—I mean the Puritans. To no man among the Puritans are the lovers of religious freedom under such large obligations as they are to Richard Baxter. This is the man, and these are the times, which form the subject of this book.[7]

I am fully sensible of the difficulties which surround the subject. It is a subject which few historians handle fairly, simply because they do not understand spiritual religion. To an unconverted man the religious differences of the day of the Puritans must necessarily

---

[6] Original: speak tonight.
[7] Original: this evening's lecture.

appear foolishness. He is no more qualified to give an opinion about them than a blind man is to talk of pictures. It is a subject which no clergyman of the Church of England can approach without laying himself open to misrepresentation. He will be suspected of disaffection to his own Church, if he speaks favorably of men who opposed bishops. But it is a subject on which it is most important for Christian young men to have distinct opinions, and I must ask for a patient hearing. If I can correct some false impressions, if I can supply you with a few great principles to guide you in these dangerous times,[8] I feel I shall have done your souls an essential service. And if I fail to interest you in Baxter and his Times, I am sure the fault is not in the subject, but in me.

---

[8] Original: these perilous times.

1

BAXTER'S TIMES

The times in which Baxter lived comprehend such a vast amount of interesting matter that I must, out of necessity, leave many points in their history entirely untouched.

You will see my meaning when I tell you that he was born in 1615, and died in 1691. Nearly all his life was passed under the dynasty of a house which reigned over England with no benefit to the country and no credit to itself—I mean the Stuarts. He lived through the reign of James I, Charles I, Charles II, and James II, and was buried in the reign of William III. He was in the prime of health and intellectual vigor all through the days of the Commonwealth and the Civil Wars. He witnessed the overthrow of the Monarchy and the Church of England, and their subsequent re-establishment. He was a contemporary of Cromwell, of Laud, of Strafford, of Hampden, of Pym, of Monk, of Clarendon, of Milton, of Hale, of Jeffreys, of Blake. In his days took place the public execution of an English monarch, Charles I, of an Archbishop of Canterbury, Laud, and of a Lord-

Lieutenant of Ireland Strafford. Within the single period of his life are to be found the plague, the fire of London, the Westminster Assembly, the Long Parliament, the Savoy Conference, and the rejection of two thousand of the best ministers of the Church of England by the Act of Uniformity. Such were the eventful times in which Baxter lived. I cannot pretend to enter fully into them. Their history forms a huge picture, like the moving panorama of the Mississippi, which it is utterly impossible to take in at a glance. I shall simply try to fix your attention on a few of the leading features of the picture, and I shall choose those points which appear to me most likely to be useful in the present day.

Moving away from the principles of the Reformation

One remarkable feature in the history of Baxter's times is the move backward from the principles of the Protestant Reformation, which commenced in his youth. Doctrines and practices began to be maintained, both by preachers and writers in the Church of England, which Latimer and Jewell would never have sanctioned. Sound evangelical teaching was decried and run down, under the specious name of Calvinism. Good bishops, like Davenant, were snubbed and reprimanded. Bad bishops, like Montague and Wren, were patted on the back and encouraged. Preaching and lecturing were depreciated, and forms and ceremonies were exalted. The benefits of episcopacy were extravagantly magnified. Candlesticks and crosses, and all manner of Popish ornaments, were introduced into some of the churches. The sanctity of the Lord's day was invaded by the abominable "Book of Sports," and common people were encouraged to spend Sunday in England as it is now spent in France. The communion-tables, which up to this time had stood in the middle of the chancel, were removed to the east end of the churches, put behind rails, and profanely called altars. Against all these sapping and mining operations, some, no doubt, protested loudly but still the sappers and miners went on.

The prime agent in the whole movement was Archbishop Laud. Whether that unhappy man really intended to reunite the Church of England with the Church of Rome is a question which will probably never be settled till the last day. One thing is very certain, that no one could have played the game of Rome more thoroughly than he did.

Like many a mischief-maker before and since, Laud pulled the house upon his own head. He raised a storm at length before which the Church, the Throne, and the Bishops, all went down together, and in the midst of which he himself was put on his trial and lost his life. But the Church of England received an injury in Laud's days from which it has never entirely recovered. Since his time there never has been lacking a succession of men among its ministers who have held most of Laud's principles, and occasionally have boldly walked in his steps. So true are the words of Shakespeare, "The evil that men do lives after them."[9]

The harm that Queen Mary did to the Church of England was nothing compared to the harm done by Laud.

Young men, never underrate the mischief that one bold, bad man can do, and especially in matters of religion. The seeds of error are like thistle-down. One head scattered by the wind will sow a whole field. One Tom Paine can rear up Infidels all over the world. One Laud can leaven generations with untold mischief. Never suppose that Tractarianism is a legitimate child of the Church of England. It is not so. It was scarcely heard of till the time of the Stuarts. Never suppose that Tractarianism is a new invention of these latter days. It is not so. It is two hundred years old. The father of Tractarians is Archbishop Laud. Remember these things, and you will have learned something from Baxter's times.

Charles I and his Parliament

Another remarkable feature in the history of Baxter's times is the famous civil war between Charles I and his Parliament.

All war is an evil—a necessary evil sometimes—but still an evil; and of all wars, the most distressing is a civil war. It is a kind of huge family quarrel. It is a struggle in which victory brings no glory, because the strife has been

---

[9] William Shakespeare, *Julius Caesar*, 3.2.4.

a strife of brethren. Edge Hill, and Newbury, and Marston Moor, and Naseby, and Worcester, are names which call up none but painful reflections. The victors in each battle had spilled the blood of their own countrymen, and lessened the general strength of the nation.

But there is a point of view in which the civil war between Charles I and his Parliament was peculiarly distressing. I allude to the striking fact, that the general irreligion and immorality of the King's party did more to ruin his cause than all the armies which the Parliament raised. There were hundreds and thousands of steady, quiet men, who, at the beginning of the war, were desirous to be still, and help neither side. But when they found that a man could not read his Bible to his dependents and have prayer in his family without being persecuted as a Roundhead,[10] they felt obliged, in self-defense, to join the Parliamentary forces. In plain words, the wickedness and profligacy of many of the Cavaliers drove godly men into the ranks of their enemies. That there was plenty of hypocrisy, fanaticism, and enthusiasm on the Parliamentary side I make no question. That there were some good men among the Cavaliers, such as Lord Falkland, I do not deny. But after every allowance, I have no doubt there was far more true

---

[10] *Roundheads* meaning those who supported Parliament of England during the English Civil War.

religion among those who fought for the Parliament than among those who fought for the King.

The result of the civil war, under these peculiar circumstances, never need surprise anyone who knows human nature. The drinking, swearing, roistering troopers, who were led by Prince Rupert, and Wilmot, and Goring, proved no match for the praying, psalm-singing, Bible reading men whom Cromwell, and Fairfax, and Ireton, and Harrison, and Fleetwood, and Desborough, brought into the field. The steadiest men will in the long run make the best soldiers. A side which has a strong religious principle among its supporters will seldom be a losing one. Those who honor God, God will honor; and they that despise Him shall be lightly esteemed.[11]

I shall dismiss the subject of the civil war with one general remark, and one caution: My general remark is that deeply as we must regret the civil war, we must in fairness remember that we probably owe to it the free and excellent Constitution which we possess in this country. God can bring good out of evil. The back and forth swinging[12] of England between despotism[13] and anarchy, and anarchy and despotism, for many years after the breach between Charles I and the House of Commons, were certainly tremendously violent. Still we must confess that great political lessons were probably

---

[11] 1 Samuel 2:30.

[12] Original: the oscillations.

[13] *Despotism* meaning to use authoritative power forcefully.

imprinted on the English mind at that period, of which we are reaping the benefit at this very day. Monarchs were taught that, like planets in the heavens above,[14] they must be content to move in a certain orbit, and that an enlightened people would not be governed and taxed without the consent of an unfettered House of Commons. Nations were taught that it is a far easier thing to pull to pieces than to build, and to upset an ancient monarchy than to find a government which shall be a satisfactory substitute. Many of the foundations of our choicest national privileges, I make no doubt, were laid in the Commonwealth times. You will do well to remember this. You may rest satisfied that this country owes an immense debt of gratitude to Brooke, and Hampden, and Whitelock, and Pym.

The caution I wish to give you respects the execution of Charles I. You will do well to remember that the great bulk of the Puritans were entirely guiltless of any participation in the trial and death of the king. It is a vulgar error to suppose, as many do, that the whole Parliamentary party are accountable for that wicked and unwise act.[15] The immense majority of the Presbyterians protested loudly against it. Baxter tells us expressly in his autobiography that together with many other ministers, he declared his abhorrence of it, and used every exertion to prevent it. The deed was the doing of

---

[14] Original: in heaven.
[15] Original: and impolitic act.

11

Cromwell and his immediate adherents in the army, and it is at their door that the whole guilt must lie. That the great body of the Puritans espoused the Parliamentary side there is no doubt. But as to any abstract dislike to royalty, or assent to King Charles' death, the Puritans are entirely innocent. Remember this, young men, and you will have learned something from the history of Baxter's times.

The rise and conduct of Oliver Cromwell

The next feature in the history of Baxter's times, to which I shall venture to call your attention, is the rise and conduct of that remarkable man, Oliver Cromwell.

There are few men on whose character more public criticism and abuse[16] has been heaped than Oliver Cromwell. He has been painted by some as a monster of wickedness and hypocrisy. Nothing has been too bad to say of him. Such an estimate of him is simply ridiculous. It defeats the end of those who form it. They forget that it is no compliment to England to suppose that it would so long tolerate the rule of such a monster. The man who could raise himself from being the son of a brewer at Huntingdon to be the most successful general of his age, and absolute dictator of this country for many years must, on the very face of facts, have been a most extraordinary man.

---

[16] Original: more obloquy has been.

For my own part I tell you frankly, that I think you ought to consider the estimate of Cromwell, which Carlyle and D'Aubigné have formed, to be a near approach to the truth. I own I cannot go the lengths of the latter writer. I dare not pronounce positively that Cromwell was a sincere Christian. I leave the question in suspense. I hazard no opinion about it one way or the other, because I do not find sufficient materials for forming an opinion. If I were to look at his private letters only, I should not hesitate to call him a converted man. But when I look at some of his public acts, I see much that appears to me very inexplicable. And when I observe how doubtfully Baxter and other good men, who were his contemporaries, speak of him, my hesitancy as to his spirituality is much increased. In short, I turn from the question in a state of doubt.

I feel no doubt at all that Oliver Cromwell was one of the greatest Englishmen that ever lived. No man ever won supreme power by the sword, and then used that power with such moderation as he did. England was probably more feared and respected throughout Europe, during the short time that he was Protector, than she ever was before, or ever has been since. His very name carried terror with it. He declared that he would make the name of an Englishman as great as ever that of a Roman had been. And he certainly succeeded. He made it publicly known that he would not allow the Protestant faith to be insulted in any part of the world. And he kept his word. When the Duke of Savoy began to persecute the Vaudois in his days, Cromwell interfered at once on their behalf, and never rested until the duke's army was recalled from the villages, and the poor people's goods and houses restored. When certain Protestants at Nismes, in France, were threatened with oppressive usage by the French government, Cromwell instructed his ambassador at Paris to insist at once,[17] that proceedings against them should be dropped, and in the event of a refusal, to leave Paris immediately. In fact, it was said that Cardinal Mazarin, the French Minister, would change countenance when Cromwell's name was mentioned; and that it was almost proverbial in France, that the Cardinal was more afraid of Cromwell than of the devil. As for the Pope, he was so dreadfully frightened by a fleet which Cromwell sent into the Mediterranean, under Blake, to settle some matters with the Duke of Tuscany, that he commanded processions to be made in Rome, and the host to be exposed for forty hours, in order to avert the judgments of God, and save the Church. In short the influence of English Protestantism was never so powerfully felt throughout Europe as it was in the days of Oliver Cromwell.

I will only ask you to remember, in addition to these facts, that Cromwell's government was remarkable for its toleration, and this too, in an age when toleration was very little understood; that his private life was irreproachable; and that he enforced a standard of

---

[17] Original: insist peremptorily.

morality throughout the kingdom which was, unhappily unknown in the days of the Stuarts. Remember all these things, and then I think you will not lightly give way to the common opinion that Cromwell was a wicked and hypocritical man. Rest assured that his character deserves far better treatment than it has generally received previously. Regard him as one who, with all his faults, did great things for England.[18] Let not those faults blind your eyes to the real greatness of his character. Give him a high place in the list of great men before your mind's eye. Do this and you will have learned something from Baxter's times.

The suicidal blindness of the Church

There is one more feature in the history of Baxter's times which I feel it impossible to pass over. I allude to the suicidal blindness of the Church of England under the Stuarts.

I touch on this subject with some reluctance. You will believe, I hope, that I love the Church, of which I am a minister, heartily and sincerely; but I have never found out that my Church lays claim to infallibility, and I am bound to confess that in the times of the Stuarts she committed some tremendous mistakes. Far be it from me to say that these mistakes were chargeable upon all her members. Abbot, and Carlton, and Davenant, and Hall, and Prideaux, and Usher, and Reynolds, and

---

[18] Original: for your country.

Wilkins, were bright exceptions among the Bishops, both as to doctrine and practice. But, unhappily, these good men were always in a minority in the Church and the manner in which the majority administered the affairs of the Church is the subject to which I wish to call your attention. You ought to know something about the subject, because it serves to throw immense light on the history of our unhappy religious divisions in England.[19] You ought to know something of it especially, because it is one which is intimately bound up with Baxter's life.

One part of the suicidal blindness of the Church, to which I have referred, was its long-continued attempt to compel conformity, and prohibit private religious exercises, by pains and penalties. A regular crusade was kept up against everybody who infringed its canons, or did anything contrary to its rubrics. Hundreds and thousands of men, for many years, were summoned before magistrates, fined, imprisoned, and often ruined; not because they had offended against the gospel or the Ten Commandments, not because they had made any open attack on the churches, but merely because they had transgressed some wretched ecclesiastical by-law, more honored in the breach than in the observance; or because they tried by quiet, private meetings, to obtain some spiritual edification over and above that which the public services of the Church provided. At one time we read of good men having their ears cut off and their

---

[19] Original: in this country.

noses slit, for writing unfavorably of bishops. This was the fate of the father of Archbishop Leighton. At another time we read of an enactment by which any one present at a meeting of five or more persons, where there was any exercise of religion in other manner than that allowed by the liturgy of the Church of England, was to be fined, or imprisoned for three months for the first offense, six months for the second offense, and for the third, transported for seven years. Many were afraid to have family prayer if more than four acquaintances were present. Some families had scruples about saying grace if five strangers were at table. Such was the state of England in the seventeenth century under the Stuarts.

The result of this miserable policy was just exactly what might have been expected. There arose a spirit of deep discontent on the part of the persecuted. There sprung up among them a feeling of disaffection to the Church in which they had been baptized, and a rooted conviction that a system must necessarily be bad in principle which could bear such fruits. Men became sick of the very name of the liturgy, when it was bound up in their memories with a fine or a jail. Men became weary of episcopacy, when they found that bishops were more frequently a terror to good works than to evil ones. The words of Baxter, in a striking passage on this subject in his autobiography, are very remarkable: "The more the bishops thought to cure schism by punishment, the more they increased the opinion that they were persecuting enemies of godliness, and the captains of the profane."

And who that knows human nature can wonder at such a state of feeling? The mass of men will generally judge an institution by its administration, more than by its abstract excellencies. When plain Englishmen saw that a man might do anything so long as he did not break an ecclesiastical canon; when they saw that people might gamble, and swear, and get drunk, and no one made them afraid, but that people who met after service to sing psalms and join in prayer were heavily punished; when they saw that godless, ignorant, reprobate, profligate spendthrifts, sat under their own vines and fig-trees in peace, so long as they conformed and went to their parish churches; but that humble, holy, conscientious, Bible-reading persons, who sometimes went out of their parishes to church, were severely fined; when they found that Charles the Second and his boon companions were free to waste a nation's substance in riotous living, while the saints of the nation, like Baxter and Jenkyn, were rotting in jails. I say, when plain Englishmen saw these things, they found it hard to love the Church which did them. Yet all this might often have been seen in many counties of England under the Stuarts. If this was not suicidal blindness on the part of the Church of England, I know not what is. It was helping the devil by driving good men out of her communion. It was literally bleeding herself to death.

The crowning piece of folly which the majority in the Church of England committed under the Stuarts, was procuring the Act of Uniformity to be enacted in the year 1662. This, you must remember, took place at the beginning of Charles the Second's reign, and shortly after the re-establishment of the monarchy and the Church.

This famous act imposed terms and conditions of holding office on all ministers of the Church of England which had never been imposed before, from the time of the Reformation. It was notoriously so framed as to be offensive to the consciences of the Puritans, and to drive them out of the Church. For this purpose it was entirely successful. Within a year, no less than two thousand clergymen resigned their livings rather than accept its terms. Many of these two thousand were the best, the ablest, and the holiest ministers of the day. Many men, who had been regularly ordained by Bishops, and spent twenty or thirty years in the service of the Church without harassing anyone,[20] was suddenly commanded to accept new conditions of holding preferment, and turned out to starve, because he refused. Sixty of the leading parishes in London were at once deprived of their ministers, and their congregations left like sheep without a shepherd. Taking all things into consideration, a more irresponsible[21] and disgraceful deed never disfigured the records[22] of a Protestant church.

It was a disgraceful deed, because it was a flat contradiction to the king's own promise at Breda, before

---

[20] Original: without molestation.

[21] Original: impolitic.

[22] Original: annals.

he came back from exile. He was brought back on the distinct understanding that the Church of England should be re-established on such a broad and liberal basis as to satisfy the conscientious scruples of the Puritans. Had it not been for the assistance of the Puritans he would never have got back at all. And yet, as soon as the reins of power were fairly in the king's hands, his promise was deliberately broken.

It was a disgraceful deed, because the great majority of the ejected ministers might easily have been retained in the Church by a few small concessions. They had no abstract objection to episcopacy, or to a liturgy. A few alterations in the prayers, and a moderate liberty in the conduct of divine worship, according to Baxter's calculation, would have satisfied sixteen hundred out of the two thousand. But the ruling party were determined not to make a single concession. They had no wish to keep the Puritans in. When someone observed to Archbishop Sheldon, the chief mover in the business, that he thought many of the Puritans would conform, and accept the Act of Uniformity, the Archbishop replied, "I am afraid they will." To show the spirit of the ruling party in the Church, they actually added to the number of apocryphal lessons in the Prayer-book calendar at this time. They made it a matter of congratulation among themselves that they had thrust out the Puritans, and got in Bel and the Dragon.[23]

It was a disgraceful deed, because the ejected ministers were, many of them, men of such ability and attainments, that great sacrifices ought to have been made in order to retain them in the Church. Baxter, Poole, Manton, Bates, Calamy, Brooks, Watson, Charnock, Caryl, Howe, Flavel, Bridge, Jenkyn, Owen, Goodwin, are names whose praise is even now in all the churches. The men who turned them out were not to be compared to them. The names of the vast majority of them are hardly known. But they had power on their side, and they were resolved to use it.

It was a disgraceful deed, because it showed the world that the leaders of the Church of England, like the Bourbons in modern times, had learned nothing and forgotten nothing during their exile. They had not forgotten the old bad ways of Laud, which had brought such misery on England. They had not learned that conciliation and concession are the most becoming graces in the rulers of a church, and that persecution, in the long run, is sure to be a losing game.

I dare not dwell longer on this point. I might easily bring forward more illustrations of this sad feature in Baxter's times. I might tell you of the infamous Oxford Act, in 1665, which forbade the unhappy ejected

---

[23] *Bel and the Dragan* is an apocryphal story added to the book of Daniel. It is not found in the Protestant Bible.

ministers to live within five miles of any corporate town, or of any place where they had formerly preached. But enough has been said to show you that when I spoke of the suicidal blindness of the Church of England, I did not speak without cause. The consequences of this blindness are manifest to anyone who knows England. The divided state of Protestantism in this country is of itself a great fact which speaks volumes.

Act of Uniformity

Against the policy of the ruling party in the Church of England, under the Stuarts, I always shall protest. I do not feel the scruples which Baxter and his ejected brethren felt about the Act of Uniformity. Much as I respect them, I think them wrong and misguided in their judgments. But I think that Archbishop Sheldon and the men who refused to go one step to meet them were far more wrong and far more misguided. I believe they did an injury to the cause of true religion in England, which will probably never be repaired by sowing the seeds of endless divisions. They were the men who laid the foundation of English dissent. I believe they recklessly threw away a golden opportunity of doing good. They might easily have made my own beloved Church far more effective and far more useful than she ever has been, by wise and timely concessions. They refused to do this and instead of a healing measure, brought forward their unhappy Act of Uniformity. I disavow any sympathy with their proceedings, and can never think of them without the deepest regret.

I cannot leave the subject of Baxter's times without offering you one piece of counsel. I advise you then not to believe everything you may happen to read on the subject of the times of the Stuarts. There are no times, perhaps, about which prejudice and party-spirit have so warped the judgment and jaundiced the eyesight of historians. If anyone want a really fair and impartial history of the times, I strongly advise him to read Marsden's *History of the Puritans.*[24] I regard these two volumes as the most valuable addition which has been made to our stock of religious history in modern times.

---

[24] J. B. Marsden, *The History of the Later Puritans: 1642–62* (London: Hamilton, Adams, & Co., 1852).

2

BAXTER'S LIFE

And now let me turn from Baxter's times to Baxter himself. Without some knowledge of the times, you would hardly understand the character and conduct of the man. A few plain facts about the man will be more likely than anything I can say to fasten in your minds the times.

Richard Baxter was the son of a small landed proprietor of Eaton Constantine, in Shropshire, and was born, in 1615, at Rowton, in the same county where Mr. Adeney, his mother's father, resided.

He seems to have been under religious impressions from a very early period of his life, and for this, under God, he was indebted to the training of a pious father. Shropshire was a very dark, ungodly county in those days. The ministers were generally ignorant, graceless, and unable to preach; and the people, as might be expected, were profligate, and despisers of them that were good. In Eaton Constantine, the parishioners spent the greater part of the Lord's day in dancing round a Maypole near old Mr. Baxter's door, to his great distress and annoyance. Yet even here grace triumphed over the world in the case of his son, and he was added to the noblest host of those who serve the Lord from their youth.

It is always interesting to observe the names of religious books when God is pleased to use them in bringing souls to the knowledge of Himself. The books which had the most effect on Baxter, were Bunny's *Resolution*;[25] Perkins' *On Repentance*,[26] *On Living and Dying Well*,[27] and *On the Government of the Tongue*;[28] Oulverwell's *On faith*; and Sibbs' *Bruised Reed*.[29] Disease and the prospect of death did much to carry on the spiritual work within him. He says in his Autobiography:

> Weakness and pain helped me to study how to die. That set me on studying how to live, and that on studying the doctrines from which I must fetch my motives and my comforts.[30]

---

[25] Edmund Bunny, *A Booke of Exercise Pertaining to Resolution* (R.P, 1584).

[26] William Perkins, *Two treatises. The first, of the nature and practise of repentance. The second, of the combate of the flesh and spirit* (London: John Legatt, 1625).

[27] William Perkins, *A Salve for a Sick Man, or a Treatise on Godliness in Sickness and Dying* (London: John Legatt, 1616).

[28] William Perkins, *On the Government of the Tongue According to God's Word* (London: John Legatt, 1597).

[29] Richard Sibbs, *The Bruised Reede, and Smoaking Flax* (London: M. F. for R. Dawlman, 1631).

[30] William Orme, *The Life and Times of the Rev. Richard Baxter*, Volume 1 (Boston: Crocker & Brewster, 1831), 16.

At the age of twenty-two he was ordained a clergyman by Thornborough, bishop of Worcester. He had never had the advantage of a university education. A free-school at Wroxeter, and a private tutor at Ludlow, had done something for him; and his own insatiable love of study had done a good deal more. He probably entered the ministry far better furnished with theological learning than most young men of his day. He certainly entered it with qualifications far better than a knowledge of Greek and Hebrew. He entered it truly moved by the Holy Spirit, and a converted man. He says himself:

> I knew that the want of academic honors and degrees were like to make me contemptible with the most. But yet, expecting to be so quickly in another world, the great concernment of miserable souls did prevail with me against all impediments. And being conscious of a thirsty desire of men's conscience and salvation, I resolved, that if one or two souls only might be won to God, it would easily recompense all the dishonor which, for want of titles, I might undergo from men.[31]

From the time of his ordination to his death, Baxter's life was a constant series of strange vicissitudes, and intense physical and mental exertions—sometimes

---

[31] *Life of the Rev. Richard Baxter,* (London: Religious Tract Society, 1832), 15.

in prosperity, and sometimes in adversity; sometimes praised and sometimes persecuted. At one period he was catechising in the lanes of Kidderminster, at another disputing with bishops in the Savoy Conference. One year he was writing the *Saint's Rest*,[32] at the point of death in a quiet country house, another year a marching chaplain to a regiment in Cromwell's army. One day he was offered a bishopric by Charles II, another day cast out of the Church by the Act of Uniformity. One year arguing for monarchy with Cromwell, and telling him it was a blessing, another day tried before Jeffreys on a charge of seditious[33] writing. One time living quietly at Acton in the society of Judge Hale, at another languishing in prison under some atrocious ecclesiastical persecution. One day having public discussions about infant baptism with Mr. Tombes in Bewdley Church, another holding the reading-desk of Amersham Church from morning to night against the theological arguments of Antinomian dragoons[34] in the gallery. Sometimes preaching the plainest doctrines, sometimes handling the most abstruse metaphysical points; sometimes writing books[35] for the learned, sometimes writing broad-sheets for the poor. Never, perhaps, did any Christian minister

---

[32] Richard Baxter, Benjamin Fawcett, *The Saints' Everlasting Rest: Or, a Treatise on the Blessed State of the Saints in Their Enjoyment of God in Heaven: to which are Added Dying Thoughts* (Edinburgh: Waugh and Innes, 1824).

[33] *Seditious* meaning provocative, causing or inciting rebellion.

[34] *Dragoons* being a mounted infantry.

[35] Original: folio.

fill so many various positions, and never, certainly, did anyone come out of them all with such an unblemished reputation. He was always suffering under incurable disease, and seldom long out of pain, always working his mind to the uttermost, and never idle for a day. He was seemingly overwhelmed with business, and yet never refusing new work, living in the midst of the most exciting scenes, and yet holding daily converse with God. He was not sufficiently a partisan to satisfy any side, and yet feared and courted by all. He was too much of a Royalist to please the Parliamentary party, and yet too much connected with the Parliament and too holy to be popular with the Cavaliers; too much of an Episcopalian to satisfy the violent portion of the Puritan body, and too much of a Puritan to be trusted by the bishops. Never, probably, did Christian man enjoy so little rest, though serving God with a pure conscience, as did Richard Baxter

Summary of Baxter's ministry

In 1638 he began his ministry, by preaching in the Upper Church at Dudley. There he continued a year. From Dudley he removed to Bridgnorth. There he continued a year and three quarters. From Bridgnorth he removed to Kidderminster. From there, after two years, he retired to Coventry, at the beginning of the Commonwealth troubles, and awaited the progress of the civil war. From Coventry, after the battle of Naseby, he joined the Parliamentary army in the capacity of regimental chaplain. He took this office in the vain hope that he might do some good among the soldiers, and counteract the ambitious designs of Cromwell and his friends. He was obliged by illness to give up his chaplaincy in 1646, and lingered for some months between life and death at the hospitable houses of Sir John Coke of Melbourne, in Derbyshire, and Sir Thomas Rous of Rouslench, in Worcestershire. At the end of 1646 he returned to Kidderminster, and there continued laboring tirelessly[36] as parish minister for fourteen years. In 1660 he left Kidderminster for London, and took an active part in promoting the restoration of Charles II, and was made one of the king's chaplains. In London, he preached successively at St. Dunstan's, Black Friars' and St. Bride's. Shortly after this he was offered the bishopric of Hereford, but thought fit to refuse it. In 1662, he was one of the two thousand ministers who were turned out of the Church by the Act of Uniformity.

Immediately after his ejection he married a wife, who seems to have been every way worthy of him, and who was spared to be his loving and faithful companion for nineteen years. Her name was Margaret Charlton, of Apley Castle, in Shropshire. After this he lived in various places in and about London: at Acton, Totteridge, Bloomsbury, and at last in Charterhouse Square. The disgraceful treatment of his enemies made it almost impossible for him to have any certain

---

[36] Original: indefatigably.

dwelling-place. Once, at this period of his life, he was offered a Scotch bishopric, or the mastership of a Scotch university, but declined both offices. With few exceptions, the last twenty-nine years of his life were embittered by repeated prosecutions, fines, imprisonment, and harassing controversies. When he could he preached, and when he could not preach he wrote books, but something he was always doing. The Revolution and accession of William III brought him some little respite from persecution, and death at last removed the good old man to that place where "the wicked cease from troubling and the weary are at rest,"[37] in the year 1691, and the seventy-sixth year of his age.

Such is a brief outline of the life of one of the most distinguished Puritans who lived under the Stuarts, and one of the most devoted ministers of the gospel this country has ever seen. It is an outline which you will readily believe might be filled up to an indefinite length. I cannot, of course, pretend to do more than call your attention to a few leading particulars. If I do not tell you more it is not from want of matter but of time. But if anyone wishes to know why Baxter's name stands so high as it does in the list of English worthies, I ask him to listen to me for a few minutes, and I will soon show him cause.

---

[37] Job 3:17.

Baxter's personal holiness

For one thing, you must know, Baxter was a man of most eminent personal holiness. Few men have ever lived before the eyes of the world for fifty or sixty years, as he did, and left so fair and unblemished a reputation. Bitterly and cruelly as many hated him, they could find no fault in the man, except as concerning the law of his God. He seems to have been holy in all the relations of life, and in all the circumstances in which man can be placed. He was holy as a son, a husband, a minister, and a friend. He was holy in prosperity and in adversity, in sickness and in health, in youth and in old age. It is a fine saying of Orme, in his admirable life of him, that he was in the highest sense, a most "unearthly" man. He lived with God, and Christ, and heaven, and death, and judgment, and eternity, continually before his eyes. He cared nothing for the good things of this world: a bishopric, with all its emoluments and honors, had no charms for him. He cared nothing for the enmity of the world: no fear of man's displeasure ever turned him an inch out of his way. He was singularly independent of man's praise or blame. He could be as bold as a lion in the presence of Cromwell, or Charles II and his bishops; and yet he could be gentle as a lamb with poor people seeking how to be saved. He could be zealous as a Crusader for the rights of conscience, and yet he was of so catholic a spirit that he loved all who loved Jesus Christ in sincerity. "Be it by Conformists or by Non-Conformists," he would say, "I rejoice that Christ is preached." He was a truly humble man. To one who wrote to him expressing admiration for his character, he replied, "You admire one you do not know: knowledge would cure your error." So fair an epistle of Christ, considering the amazing trials of patience he had to go through, this country has seldom seen as Richard Baxter.

Young men, I charge you to remember this point in Baxter's character. No argument has such lasting power with the world as a holy and consistent life. Remember that this holiness was attained by a man of like passions with yourselves. Let Baxter be an encouragement and an example. Remember the Lord God of Baxter is not changed.

Baxter's powerful preaching

For another thing, Baxter was one of the most powerful preachers that ever addressed an English Congregation. He seems to have possessed all the gifts which are generally considered to make a perfect master of assemblies. He had an amazing fluency, an enormous store of matter, a most clear and lucid style, an unlimited command of forcible language; a pithy, pointed, emphatic way of presenting truth. He had a singularly moving and pathetic voice—and an earnestness of manner which swept everything before it like a torrent. He used to say, "It must be serious preaching which will make men serious in hearing and obeying it."

Two well-known lines of his show you the man: "I'll preach as though I never should preach again, and as a dying man to dying men." Dr. Bates, a contemporary, says of him:

> He had a marvelous felicity and copiousness in speaking. There was a noble negligence in his style. His great mind could not stoop to the affected eloquence of words. He despised flashy oratory. But his expressions were so clear and powerful, so convincing to the understanding, so entering into the soul, so engaging the affections, that those were as deaf as an adder who were not charmed by so wise a charmer.[38]

The effects that his preaching produced were those which such preaching always has produced and always will. As it was under the pulpit of Latimer and Whitefield, so it was under the pulpit of Baxter. At Dudley, the poor nailers would not only crowd the church, but even hang upon the windows and the leads without. At Kidderminster, it became necessary to build five new galleries, in order to accommodate the congregation. In London, the crowds who attended his ministry were so large, that it was sometimes dangerous, and often impossible, to be one of his hearers.

Once when he was about to preach at St. Lawrence Jewry, he sent word to Mr. Vines the minister, that the Earl of Suffolk and Lord Broghill were coming in a coach

---

[38] William Bates, *A Funeral-sermon for the Reverend, Holy and Excellent Divine, Mr. Richard Baxter, Who Deceased Decemb. 8. 1691. With an Account of His Life* (London: Brab. Alymer, 1692), 90–91.

with him, and would be glad to have seats. But when he and his noble companions reached the door, the crowd had so little respect for persons, that the two peers had to go home again because they could not get within hearing. Mr. Vines himself was obliged to get up into the pulpit, and sit behind the preacher, from want of room; and Baxter actually preached standing between Mr. Vines' feet.

On another occasion, when he was preaching to an enormous crowd in St. Dunstan's, Fleet Street, he made a striking use of an incident which took place during the sermon. A piece of brick fell down in the steeple, and an alarm was raised that the church, an old and rotten building, was falling. Scarcely was the alarm allayed, when a bench, on which some people were standing, broke with their weight, and the confusion was worse than ever. Many crowded to the doors to get out, and all were in a state of panic. One old woman was heard loudly asking God forgiveness for having come to the church at all, and promising, if she only got out safe, never to come there again. In the midst of all the confusion Baxter alone was calm and unmoved. As soon as order was restored, he rose and said:

> We are in the service of God to prepare ourselves that we may be fearless at the great noise of the dissolving world, when the heavens

shall pass away, and the elements melt with fervent heat.[39]

This was Baxter all over. This was the kind of thing he had not only grace, but gifts and nerve, to do. He always spoke like one who saw God, and felt death at his back. Such a man will seldom fail to preach well. Such a man will seldom be in want of hearers. Such a man deserves to be embalmed in the memory of all who want to know what God can do for a child of Adam by his Spirit. Such a man deserves to be praised.

Baxter's success

For another thing, you must know, that Baxter was one of the most successful pastors of a parish and congregation that ever lived. When he came to Kidderminster, he found it a dark, ignorant, immoral, irreligious place, containing, perhaps, three thousand inhabitants. When he left it at the end of fourteen years, he had completely turned the parish upside down. "The place before his coming," says Dr. Bates, "was like a piece of dry and barren earth; but, by the blessing of Heaven upon his labor, the face of Paradise appeared there. The bad were changed to good, and the good to

---

[39] Richard Baxter, *Memoirs of Margaret Baxter: Daughter of Francis Charlton and Wife of Richard Baxter: with Some Account of Her Mother, Mrs. Hanmer, Including a True Delineation of Her Character* (London: Richard Evans, 1826), 61.

better."[40] The number of his regular communicants averaged six hundred. "Of these," Baxter tells us, "there were not twelve of whom I had not good hope as to their sincerity."

The Lord's day was thoroughly reverenced and observed. It was said, "You might have heard a hundred families singing psalms and repeating sermons as you passed through the streets." When he came there, there was about one family in a street which worshiped God at home. When he went away, there were some streets in which there was not more than one family on a side that did not do it and this was the case even with inns and public-houses. Even of their religious families, there were very few which had not some converted relations. Some of the poor people became so well versed in theology, that they understood the whole body of divinity, and were able to judge difficult controversies. Some were so able in prayer, that few ministers could match them in order, fullness, apt expressions, holy oratory and fervor. Best of all, the temper of their minds and the innocency of their lives were much more commendable[41] even than their gifts.

Baxter's pastoral skill

The grand instrument to which Baxter used to attribute this astounding success was his system of household

---

[40] William Bates, *Funeral Sermon*, 88.
[41] Original: laudable.

visitation and regular private conference with his parishioners. No doubt this did immense good, and the more so because it was a new tiling in those days. Nevertheless, there is no denying the fact that the most elaborate parochial machinery of modern times has never produced such effects as those you have just heard of at Kidderminster. And the true account of this I believe to be, that no parish has ever had such a wonderful mainspring in the middle of it as Baxter was. While some divines were wrangling about the divine right of Episcopacy or Presbytery, or splitting hairs about reprobation and free-will, Baxter was always visiting from house to house, and beseeching men, for Christ's sake, to be reconciled to God[42] and flee from the wrath to come.[43] While others were entangling themselves in politics, and burying their dead amid the potsherds of the earth, Baxter was living a crucified life and daily preaching the gospel. I suspect he was the best and wisest pastor that an English parish has ever had, and a model that many of us would do well to follow. Once more I say, have I not a right to tell you such a polished instrument as this ought not to be allowed to rust in oblivion? Such a man as this deserves to be praised.

---

[42] 2 Corinthians 5:20.
[43] Matthew 3:7; Luke 3:7.

Baxter's diligence as a writer

For another thing, you must know that Baxter was one of the most diligent theological writers the world has ever seen. Few have the slightest idea of the immense number of works in divinity which he wrote in the fifty years of his active life. It is reckoned that they would fill sixty octavo volumes, comprising not less than thirty-five thousand closely printed pages. These works, no doubt, are not air of equal merit, and many of them probably will never repay perusal. Like the ships from Tarshish, they contain not only gold, and silver, and ivory, but also a large mass of apes and peacocks. Still, after every deduction, the writings of Baxter generally contain a great mass of solid truths, and truths often handled in a most striking and masterly way. Dr. Barrow, no mean judge, says, "That his practical writings were never mended, and his controversial ones seldom confuted." Bishop Wilkins declares, "That he had cultivated every subject he had handled—that if he had lived in the primitive times he would have been one of the fathers of the Church, and that it was enough for one age to produce such a man as Mr. Baxter." That great and good man, William Wilberforce, says, "His practical writings are a treasury of Christian wisdom;" and he adds, "I must beg to class among the brightest ornaments of the Church of England this great man, who was so shamefully ejected from the Church in 1662."

No one man has certainly ever written three such books as Baxter's three masterpieces, *The Saint's Rest,*

The Reformed Pastor,[44] and *The Call to the Unconverted*.[45] I believe they have been made blessings to thousands of souls, and are alone sufficient to place the author in the foremost rank of theological writers. Of *the Call to the Unconverted*, twenty thousand were printed in one year. Six brothers were converted at one time by reading it. Eliot, the missionary thought so highly of it, that he translated it into the Indian language, the first book after the Bible.[46] And really, when you consider that all Baxter's writings were composed in the midst of intense labor, and fierce persecution, and often under the pressure of heavy bodily disease, the wonder is not only that he wrote so much, but that so much of what he wrote should be so good. Such wonderful diligence and redemption of time the world has never seen. Once more I say, have I not a right to tell you such a man deserves to be praised?

Baxter's patience under undeserved persecution

For another thing, you must know that Baxter was one of the most patient martyrs for conscience sake, that England has ever seen. Of course, I do not mean that he was called upon to seal his faith with his blood, as our

---

[44] Richard Baxter, *The Reformed Pastor: Shewing the Nature of the Pastoral Work* (London: Robert White, 1657).

[45] Richard Baxter, *A Call to the Unconverted, to Turn and Live: And Accept of Mercy, While Mercy May be Had: as Ever They Will Find Mercy, in the Day of Their Extremity, from the Living God* (York: Wilson, Spence, and Mawman, 1791).

[46] John Eliot (c. 1604—1690).

Protestant Reformers were. But there is such a thing as wearing out the saints of the Most High by persecutions and prisons, as well as shedding the blood of the saints. There is a dying daily, which, to some natures, is worse even than dying at the stake. If anything tries faith and patience, I believe it to be the constant dropping of such wearing persecution as Baxter had to endure for nearly the last twenty-nine years of his life. He had robbed no one. He had murdered no one. He had injured no one. He held no heresy. He believed all the articles of the Christian faith. And yet no thief or felon in the present day was ever so shamefully treated as this good man. To tell you how often he was summoned, fined, silenced, imprisoned, driven from one place to another, would be an endless task. To describe all the hideous perversions of justice to which he was subjected, would be both painful and unprofitable. I will only allow myself to give one instance, and that shall be his trial before Chief Justice Jeffreys.

Baxter was tried before Jeffreys in 1685, at Westminster Hall, on a charge of having published seditious[47] matter, reflecting on the Bishops, in a paraphrase on the New Testament, which he had recently brought out. A more unfounded charge could not have been made. The book still exists,[48] and any one will see at a glance that the alleged seditious passages do

---

[47] *Seditious* meaning to cause rebellion to authority.
[48] Original: is still extant.

not prove the case. Fox, in his history of James II's reign, tells us plainly, that "the real motive for bringing him to trial was the desire of punishing an eminent dissenting teacher, whose reputation was high among his sect, and who was supposed to favor the political opinions of the Whigs."

A long and graphic account of the trial was drawn up by a bystander, and it gives so vivid a picture of the administration of justice in Baxter's days, that it may be useful to give a few short extracts from it.

From the very opening of the trial it was clear which way the verdict was intended to go. The Lord Chief Justice behaved as if he were counsel for the prosecution, and not judge. He condescended to use abusive language toward the defendant, such as was more suited to Billingsgate[49] than a court of law. One after another the counsel for the defense were brow-beaten, silenced, and put down, or else interrupted by violent verbal abuses[50] against Baxter. At one time the Lord Chief Justice exclaimed: "This is an old rogue, who has poisoned the world with his Kidderminster doctrine. He encouraged all the women and maids to bring their bodkins and thimbles to carry on war against the King of ever blessed memory. An old schismatical knave! A hypocritical villain!"

---

[49] A London fish market known for where vulgar and abusive language could often be heard.

[50] Original: violent invectives.

By-and-by he called Baxter "an old block head, an unthankful villain, a conceited, stubborn, fanatical dog. Hang him!" he said, "this one old fellow has cast more reproaches on the constitution and discipline of our Church than will be wiped off for this hundred years. But I'll handle him for it, for he deserves to be whipped through the city."[51]

Shortly afterward, when Baxter began to say a few words on his own behalf, Jeffreys stopped him, crying out: "Richard, Richard, do you think we'll hear you poison the Court? Richard, you are an old fellow, an old knave; you have written books enough to load a cart, everyone as full of sedition—I might say treason, as an egg is full of meat. Had you been whipped out of your writing trade forty years ago, it had been happy. You pretended to be a preacher of the gospel of peace, and you have one foot in the grave; it is time for you to think what kind of an account you intend to give. But leave you to yourself and I see you will go on as you have begun! but, by the grace of God, I will look after you. I know you have a mighty party, and I see a great many of the brotherhood in corners, waiting to see what will become of this mighty dove; but, by the grace of God Almighty, I'll crush you all! Come, what do you say for yourself, you old knave? Come, speak up!"[52]

---

[51] William Orme, *The Life and Times,* I, 324.

[52] Orme, *The Life and Times,* I, 326.

All this, and much more of the same kind, and even worse, went on at Baxter's trial. The extracts I have given form but a small portion of the whole account.

It is needless to say, that in such a court as this Baxter was at once found guilty. He was fined five hundred marks, which it was known he could not pay—condemned to lie in prison till he paid it, and bound over to good behavior for seven years. And the issue of the matter was, that this poor, old, diseased, childless widower, of seventy years,[53] lay for two years in Southwark jail.

It is needless, I hope, to tell you, in the year 1853, that such a trial as this was a disgrace to the judicial bench of England, and a still greater disgrace to those persons with whom the information originated, understood commonly to have been Sherlock and L'Estrange. Thank God! I trust England, at any rate, has bid a long farewell to such trials as these, whatever may be done in Italy! Wretched, indeed, is that country where low, sneaking informers are encouraged—where the terrors of the law are directed more against holiness, and Scriptural religion, and freedom of thought, than against vice and immorality; and where the seat of justice is used for the advancement of political purposes, or the gratification of petty ecclesiastical spite!

But it is right that you should know that under all this foul injustice and persecution, Baxter's grace and

---

[53] Original: threescore years and ten.

patience never failed him. "These things," he said, in Westminster Hall, "will surely be understood one day, what fools one sort of Protestants are made to persecute the other." When he was reviled, he reviled not again. He returned blessing for cursing, and prayer for ill-usage. Few martyrs have ever glorified God so much in their one day's fire as Richard Baxter did for twenty years under the ill usage of the so-called Protestants! Once more, I say, have I not a right to tell you such a man as this deserves to be remembered? Such a man deserves to be praised.

And now I hope you will consider I have proved my case. I trust you will allow that there are men who lived in times long gone by, whose character it is useful to review, and that Baxter is undeniably one of them—a real man—a true spiritual hero.

I do not ask you to regard him as a perfect and faultless being, any more than Cranmer, or Calvin, or Knox, or Wesley. I do not at all defend some of Baxter's doctrinal statements. He tried to systematize things which cannot be systematized, and he failed. You will not find such a clear, full gospel in his writings, as in those of Owen, and Bridge, and Traill. I do not think he was always right in his judgment. I regard his refusal of a bishopric as a huge mistake. By that refusal he rejected a glorious opportunity of doing good. Had Baxter been on the episcopal bench, and in the House of Lords, I do not believe the Act of Uniformity would ever have passed.

But, in a world like this you must take true Christians as they are, and be thankful for what they are. It is not given to mortal man to be faultless. Take Baxter for all together, and there are few English ministers of the gospel whose names deserve to stand higher than his. Some have excelled him in some gifts, and some in others. But it is seldom that so many gifts are to be found united in one man as they are in Baxter. Eminent personal holiness—amazing power as a preacher—unrivaled pastoral skill—indefatigable diligence as a writer—meekness and patience under undeserved persecution—all meet together in the character of this one man. Place him high in your list of great and good men. Give him the honor he deserves. Reckon it no small thing to be the fellow-countryman of Richard Baxter.

Obligation to Baxter

And here let me remark that few bodies of men are under greater obligation to Baxter and his friends than the body I have the honor to address this night—the Young Men's Christian Association.

You are allowed to associate together upon evangelical principles, and for religious ends, and no one hinders you. You are allowed to meet in large numbers, and take sweet counsel with one another, and strengthen one another's hands in the service of Christ, and no one interferes to prevent you. You are allowed to assemble for devotional purposes, to read the Word of God, and stir one another up to perseverance in the faith, in the midst of this great Babylon, and no one dares to prohibit you. How great are all these privileges! How incalculable the benefit of union, conference, sympathy, and encouragement to a young man launching forth on the stormy waters of this great city! Happy are the cities where such institutions exist! Happy are the young men whom God inclines to join them! Blessed is the labor of those by whose care and attention these institutions are kept together! They are sowing precious seed. They may sow with much toil and discouragement, but they may be sure they are sowing seed which shall yet bear fruit after many days.

But never, never forget to whom you are indebted for all this liberty of conference and association which you enjoy. Never forget that there was a time when informers would have tracked all your steps—when constables and soldiers would have rudely broken up your gatherings at Gresham Street, Saville Row, and Exeter Hall, and when your proceedings would have entailed upon you pains, penalties, fines, and imprisonments. Never forget that the happy and profitable freedom which you enjoy was only won by long-continued and intense struggles, by the blood and sufferings of noble-minded men, of whom the world was not worthy;[54] and never forget that the men who won this freedom for you was those much-abused men—the Puritans.

---

[54] Hebrews 11:38.

Yes! you all owe a debt to the Puritans, which, I trust, you will never refuse to acknowledge. You live in days when many are disposed to run them down. As you travel through life, you will often hear them derided and abused as seditious, rebellious levelers in the things of Caesar, and ignorant, fanatical, hypocritical enthusiasts in the things of God. You will often hear some semi-Popish stripling, fresh from Oxford, puffed up with new-fledged views of what he calls "apostolical succession," and proud of a little official authority, depreciating and sneering at the Puritans, as men alike destitute of learning and true religion, while, in reality, he is scarcely worthy to sit at their feet, and carry their books. To all such calumnies and false statements, I trust you will never give heed.

Settle it down in your minds that for sound doctrine, spirituality, and learning combined, the Puritans stand at the head of English divines. Settle it down in your minds, that, with all their faults, weaknesses, and defects, they alone kept the lamp of pure, evangelical religion burning in this country in the times of the Stuarts—they alone prevented Laud's Popish inclinations carrying England back into the arms of Rome. Settle it down in your minds that they fought the battle of religious freedom, of which we are reaping such fruits—that they crushed the wretched spirit of inquisitorial persecution which misguided high-Churchmen tried to introduce into this land. Give them the honor they deserve. Suffer no man to speak lightly of them in your presence. Remember your obligations to them. Reverence their memory. Stand up boldly for their reputation. Never be afraid to plead their cause. It is the cause of pure, evangelical religion. It is the cause of an open Bible, and liberty to meet, and read, and pray together. It is the cause of liberty of conscience. All these are bound up with Baxter and the Puritans. Remember this, and give them their due.

Baxter's last days

And now let me conclude this lecture by telling you that Baxter's last days were almost as remarkable as any in his life. He went down to his grave as calmly and peacefully as the setting sun in summer. His deathbed was a glorious deathbed indeed.

I like to know how great men die. I am not satisfied with knowing that men are great in the plenitude of riches and honor. I want to know whether they were great in view of the tomb. I do not want merely to know how men meet kings, and bishops, and parliaments; I want to know how they meet the king of terrors, and how they feel in the prospect of standing before the King of kings. I suspect that greatness which forsakes a man at last. I like to know how great men die, and I may be allowed, I hope, to dwell for a few moments on Baxter's death.

Few deathbeds, perhaps, were ever more truly instructive than that of this good old Puritan. His friend, Dr. Bates, has given a full description of it, and I think a few facts drawn from it may prove a suitable conclusion to this work.[55]

Baxter's last illness found him quietly living in Charterhouse Square, close to the meeting house of his friend, Dr. Sylvester. Here for the four years preceding his death, he was allowed to enjoy great quietness. The liberty of preaching the things concerning the Lord Jesus Christ, no man forbidding him, was at length fully conceded. "Here," says Dr. Calamy, "he used to preach with great freedom about another world, like one that had been there, and was come as a sort of express to make a report of it." The storm of persecution was at length over. The winds and waves that had so long burst over him were at last lulled. The saintly old Puritan was mercifully allowed to go down to the banks of Jordan in a great calm.

He continued to preach so long, notwithstanding his wasted body, that the last time he almost died in the pulpit. When disease compelled him to give over his beloved work, and take to his dying bed, it found him the same man that he had been for fifty years. His last hours were spent in preparing others and himself to meet God. He said to the friends who visited him: "You come here to learn to die. I am not the only person that must go this way. Have a care of this vain and deceitful world, and the lust of the flesh. Be sure you choose God for your portion, heaven for your home, God's glory for your end,

---

[55] Original: evening's lecture.

God's Word for your rule, and then you need never fear but we shall meet again with comfort."[56]

Never was penitent sinner more humble, and never was sincere believer more calm and comfortable. He said, "God may justly condemn me for the best duty I ever did; and all my hopes are from the free mercy of God in Christ." He had often said before, "I can more readily believe that God will forgive me, than I can forgive myself."

After a slumber, he waked saying, "I shall rest from my labors." A minister present said, "And your works will follow you." He replied, "No works; I will leave out works, if God will grant me the other." When a friend comforted him with the remembrance of the good many had received from his writings, he replied, "I was but a pen in God's hand, and what praise is due to a pen?"

When extremity of pain made him long for death, he would check himself and say, "It is not fit for me to prescribe: when you will—what you will—how you will!" Being in great anguish, he said, "How unsearchable are his ways!" and then he said to his friends, "do not think the worse of religion for what you see me suffer."

Being often asked by his friend how it was with his inward man, he replied, "I have a well-grounded assurance of my eternal happiness, and great peace and

---

[56] John Hamilton Davies, *The Life of Richard Baxter of Kidderminster: Preacher and Prisoner* (London: W. Kent and Co., 1887), 445.

comfort within; but it is my trouble that I cannot triumphantly express it, by reason of extreme pain." He added, "Flesh must perish, and we must feel the perishing; and though my judgment submit, sense will make me groan."

Being asked by a nobleman whether he had great joy from his believing apprehension of the invisible state, he replied, "What else, think you, Christianity serves for?" And then he added: "that the consideration of the Deity, in his glory and greatness, was too high for our thoughts; but the consideration of the Son of God in our nature, and of the saints in heaven whom we knew and loved, did much sweeten and familiarize heaven to him."[57]

The description of heaven in the 12th chapter of Hebrews, beginning with the "innumerable company of angels," and ending with "Jesus the Mediator, and the blood of sprinkling," was very comfortable to him. "That Scripture," he said, "deserves a thousand thousand thoughts!" And then he added, "Oh! how comfortable is that promise, 'Eye has not seen, nor ear heard, neither has it entered into the heart of man to conceive, the things God has laid up for them that love Him!'" (1 Cor. 2:9).[58] At another time he said: "That he found great comfort and sweetness in repeating the words of the Lord's Prayer, and was sorry that some good men were prejudiced against the use of it; for there

---

[57] Leonard Bacon, *Select Practical Writings of Richard Baxter*, (New Haven: Durrie & Peck, 1835), I, 222.

[58] William Bates, *Funeral Sermon*, 127–128.

were all necessary petitions for soul and body contained in it."[59]

He gave excellent counsel to young ministers who visited him on his deathbed. He used to pray earnestly "that God would bless their labors, and make them very successful in converting many souls to Christ."[60] He expressed great joy in the hope that God would do a great deal of good by them, and that they would be of moderate, peaceful spirits.

He did not forget the world he was leaving. He frequently prayed "that God would be merciful to this miserable, distracted world; and that he would preserve his Church and interest in it."[61]

He advised his friends "to beware of self-consciousness as a sin likely to ruin this nation." Being asked at the same time whether he had altered his mind in controversial points, he replied, "Those that please may know my mind in my writings. What I have done was not for my own reputation, but the glory of God."[62]

The day before he died, Dr. Bates visited him; and on his saying some words of comfort, he replied, "I have pain—there is no arguing against sense; but I have peace—I have peace!" Bates told him he was going to his long-desired home. He answered, "I believe—I

---

[59] William Bates, *Funeral Sermon*, 128.
[60] William Bates, *Funeral Sermon*, 128.
[61] William Bates, *Funeral Sermon*, 129.
[62] William Bates, *Funeral Sermon*, 129.

believe!"[63] He expressed great willingness to die. During his sickness, when the question was asked how he did, his reply was, "Almost well!" or else, "Better than I deserve to be, but not so well as I hope to be." His last words were addressed to Dr. Sylvester, "The Lord teach you how to die!"[64]

On Tuesday the 8th of December, 1691, Baxter's warfare was accomplished; and at length he entered what he had so beautifully described—the saint's everlasting rest.

He was buried at Christchurch, amid the tears of many who knew his worth, if the world and the Established Church of that day did not. The funeral was that kind of funeral which is above all in real honor: "devout men carried him to his grave, and made great lamentation over him."

He left no family, but he left behind him hundreds of spiritual sons and daughters. He left works which are still owned by God in every part of the world to the awakening and edification of immortal souls. Thousands, I doubt not, will stand up in the morning of the resurrection, and thank God for the grace and gifts bestowed on the old Puritan of Shropshire. He left a name which must always be dear to every lover of holiness, and every friend of religious liberty. No Englishman, perhaps, ever exemplified the one, or

---

[63] William Bates, *Funeral Sermon*, 130.
[64] William Orme, *The Life and Times*, I, 355.

promoted the other, more truly and really than did Richard Baxter.

Conclusion

Let me conclude by quoting the last paragraph of Dr. Bates' funeral sermon on the occasion of Baxter's death:

> Blessed be the gracious God, that he was pleased to prolong the life of his servant, so useful and beneficial to the world, to a full age, and that he brought him slowly and safely to heaven. I shall conclude this account with my own deliberate wish: May I live the short remainder of my life as entirely to the glory of God as he lived; and when I shall come to the period of my life, may I die in the same blessed peace wherein he died; may I be with him in the kingdom of light and love forever.[65]

---

[65] William Bates, *Funeral Sermon,* 131.

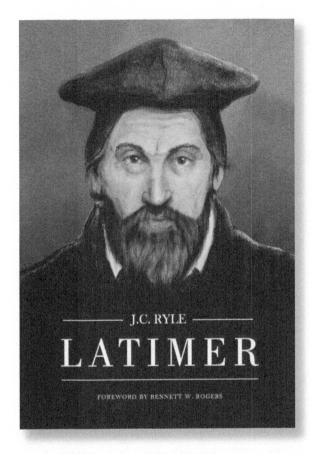

ISBN: 978-1-77526-338-8

Another of J.C Ryle's short biographies on a man of God worthy of study. In this work he briefly examines the life and work of Bishop Hugh Latimer.

MATTHEW HENRY

A CHURCH
IN THE HOUSE

Foreword by Joseph C. Harrod

ISBN: 978-1-77526-333-3

Matthew Henry exhorts fathers to lead their homes well in family worship. This is an excellent resource for those who are aiming to be faithful in family discipleship.

Fuller SERIES

Backslider

ANDREW FULLER

Foreword by: Michael A.G. Haykin

ISBN: 978-1-77526-334-0

Fuller deals with the issue of backsliding: when genuine Christians lose their passion for Christ and his kingdom. This was not a theoretical issue for Fuller, therefore, and his words, weighty when he first wrote them, are still worthy of being pondered—and acted upon.

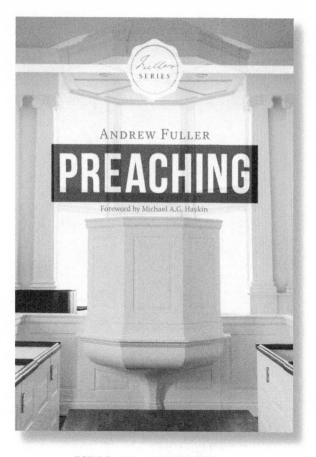

ISBN: 978-1-77526-336-4

Fuller wrote to encourage a young minister in sermon preparation and reading this work will be of great value to any preacher today.

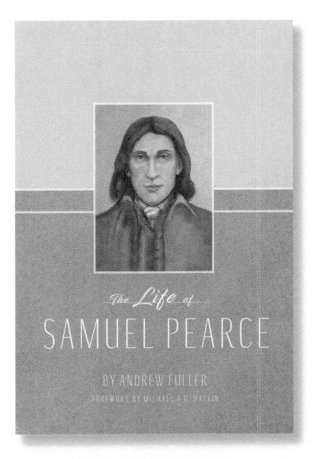

ISBN: 978-1-77526-339-5

In the eyes of Fuller, Samuel Pearce (1766–1799) was the epitome of the spirituality of their community. In fact, in that far-off day of the late eighteenth century Pearce was indeed well known for the anointing that attended his preaching and for the depth of his spirituality. It was said of him that "his ardour ... gave him a kind of ubiquity; as a man and a preacher, he was known, he was felt everywhere."

Date Completed	Name

■≡H&E *Publishing*

WWW.HESEDANDEMET.COM

ABOUT
H&E Publishing

H&E Publishing is a Canadian evangelical publishing company located out of Peterborough, Ontario. We exist to provide Christ-exalting, Gospel-centred, and Bible-saturated content aimed to show God to be as glorious and worthy as He truly is.

We seek to provide rich resources that will equip, nourish, and refresh the Christian's soul. We desire to make available a variety of works that serve this purpose in the church. One key area of focus is to revive evangelicals of the past through updated reprints.

Notes:

Notes:

Notes:

Notes:

Notes:

Notes:

Notes:

Notes:

Notes:

Notes:

Notes:

Notes:

Notes:

Notes:

Notes:

Notes:

Notes:

Notes:

Notes:

Notes:

Made in United States
North Haven, CT
10 March 2023

33843332R00061